11 Things to Tell Myself Before Bedtime

Leah Broyde Abrahams   **Ruth Broyde Sharone**

Published by: Global Peace Publications
www.LeahAbrahamsPhotography.com

Author: Ruth Broyde Sharone, www.11thingstocelebrate.com
Photographer: Cover and internal photographs by Leah Broyde Abrahams
Cover design and book design by Jason Davis
Manufactured in the United States of America.

First Edition

10 9 8 7 6 5 4 3 2 1

Paperback ISBN: 978-0-9992563-2-9

This is the second book in an 11-book inspirational series planned by Global Peace Publications.
The first was *11 Things to Celebrate Before Breakfast*

*To our parents, Raya and Samuel Broyde,
who taught us to live life with passion.*

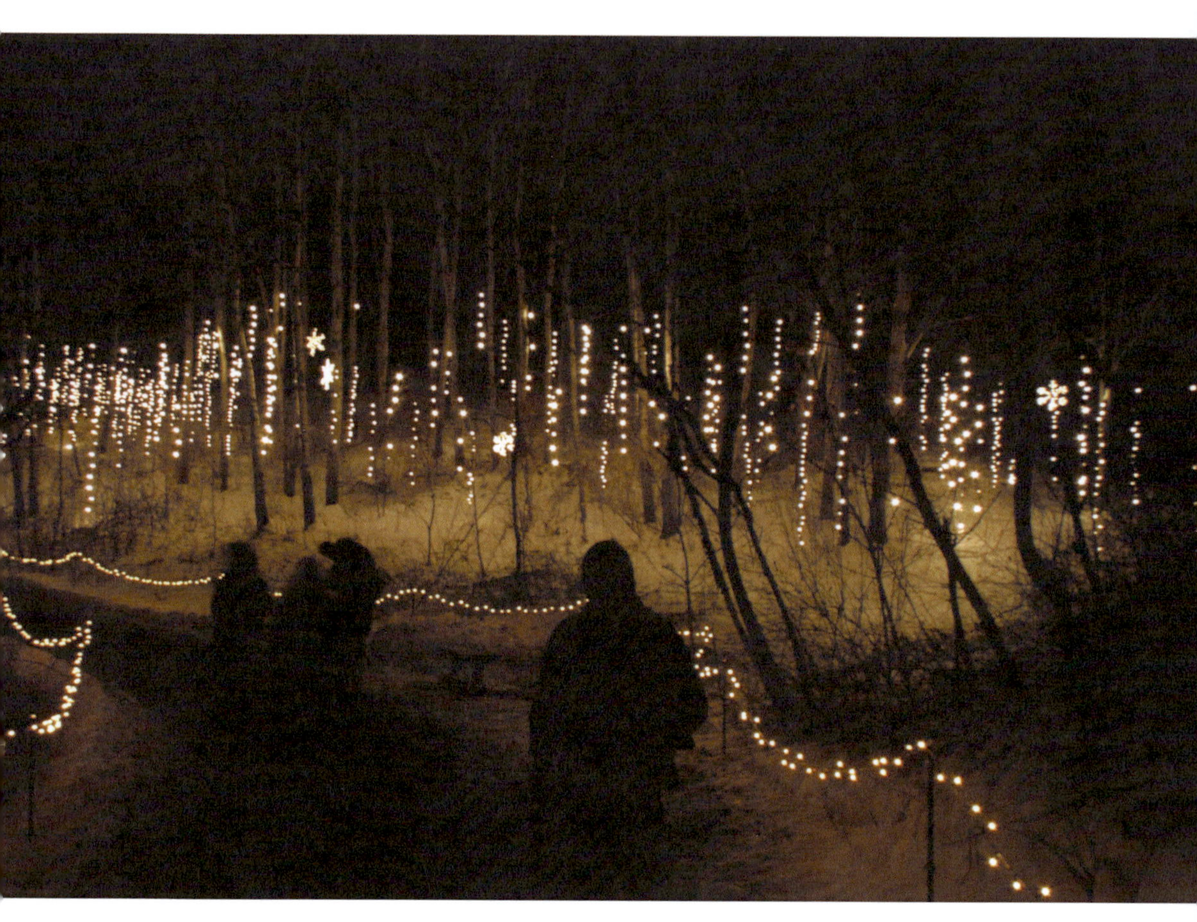

Night is a magical time.

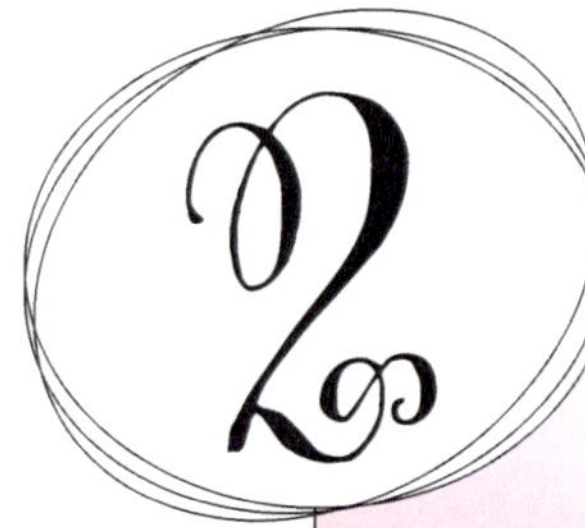

I am more grateful today
than I was yesterday.

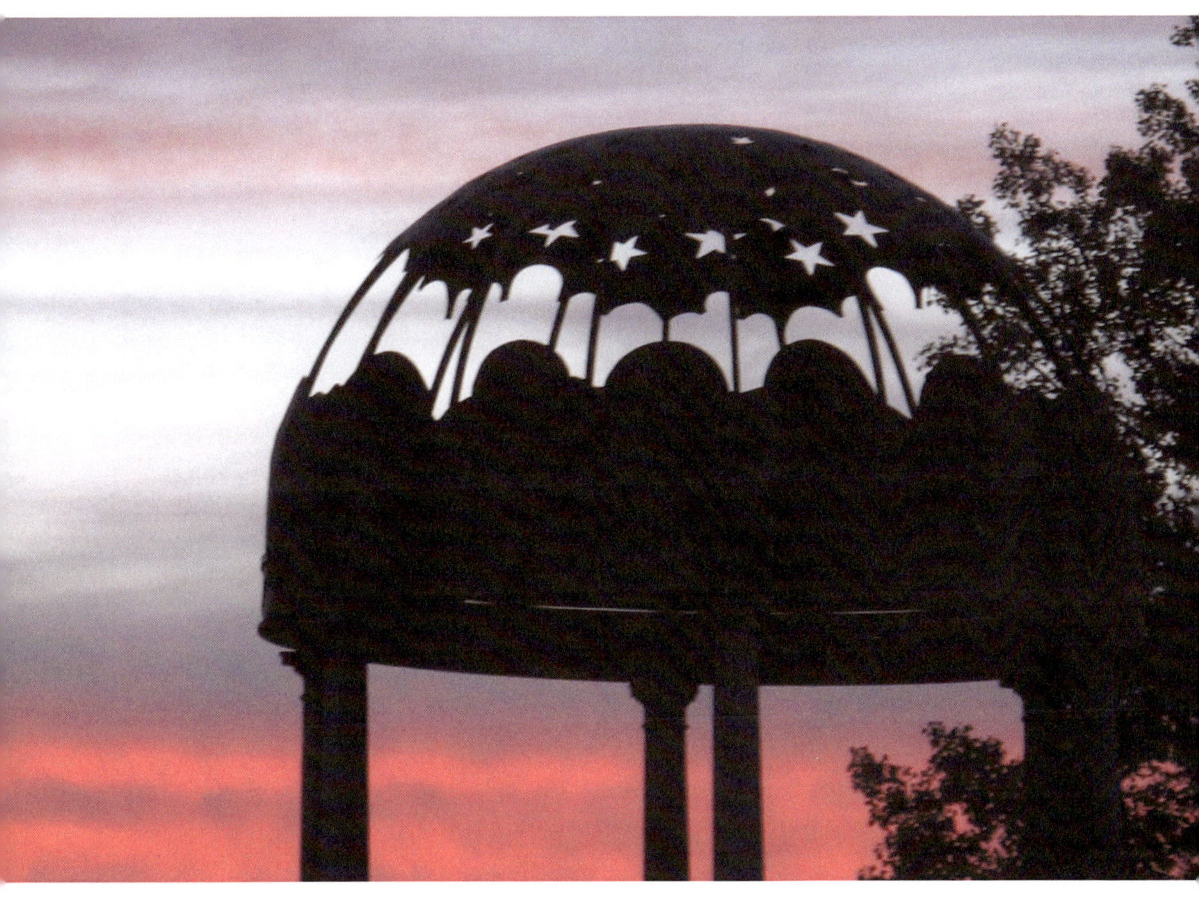

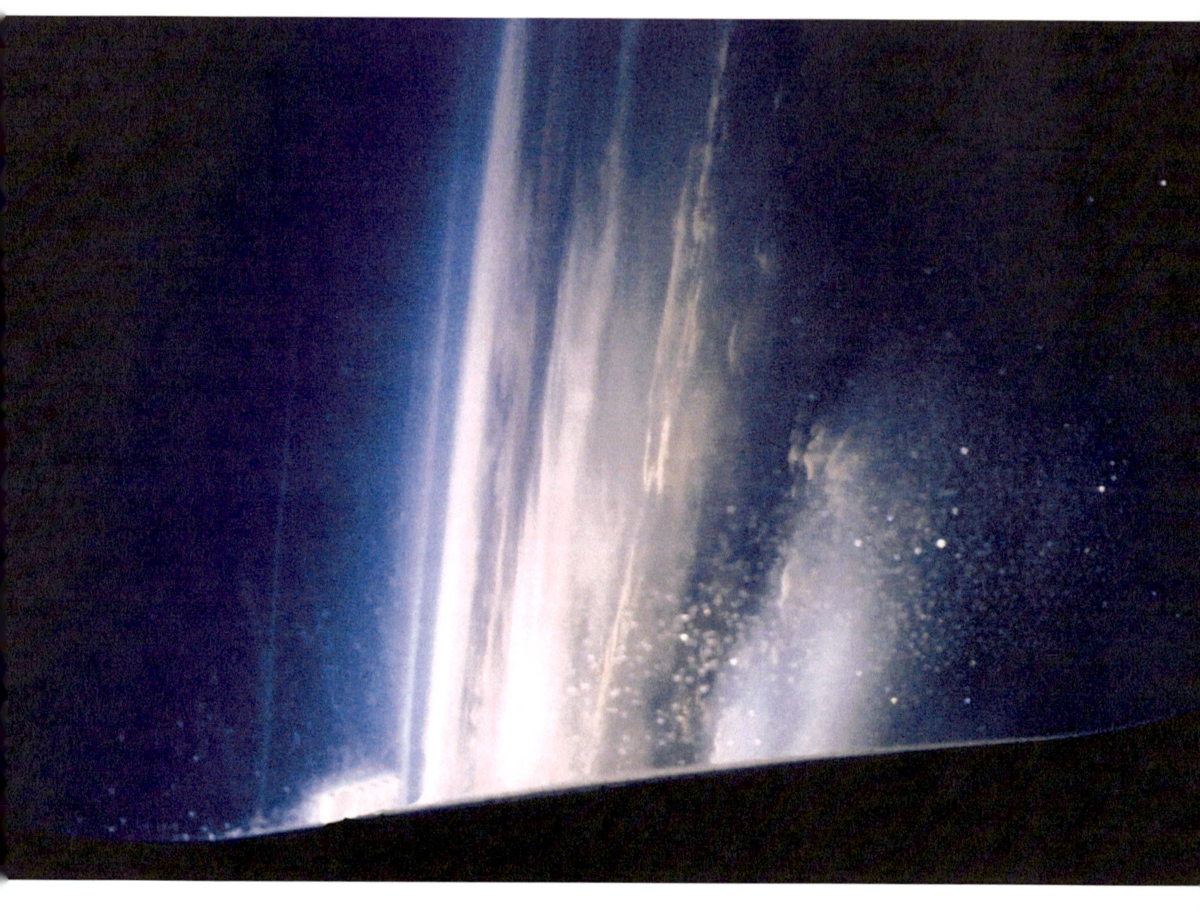

I am glad to be alive.

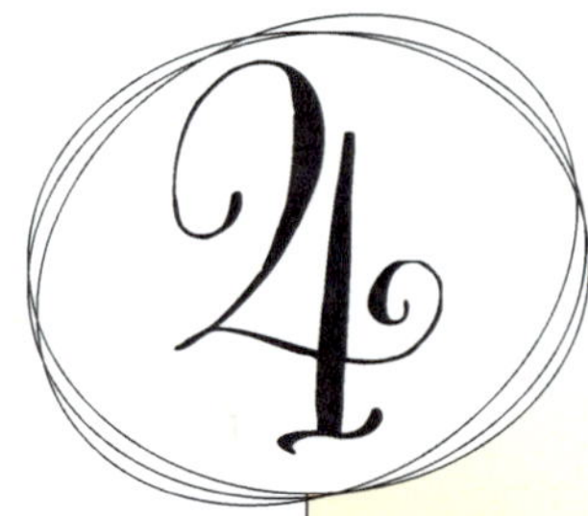

I feel loved even when
I am alone.

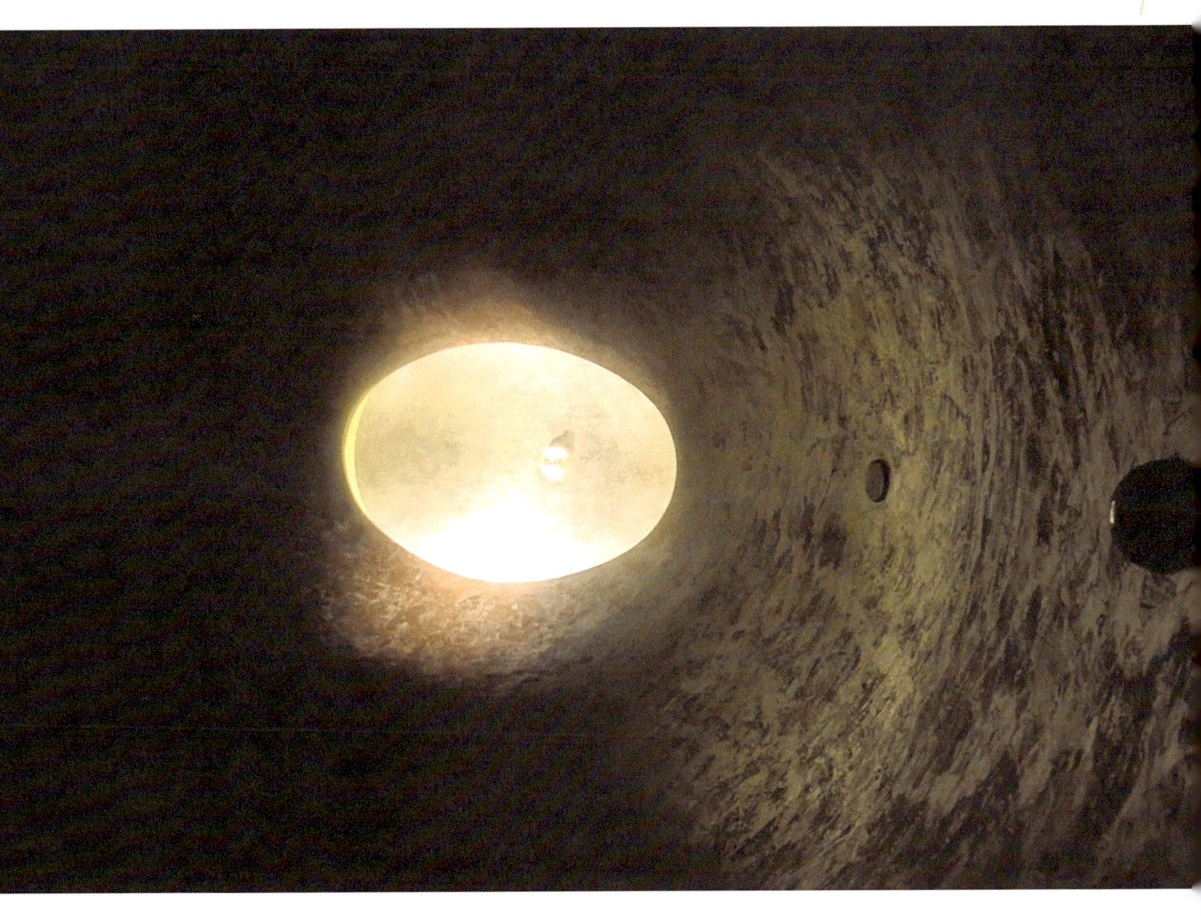

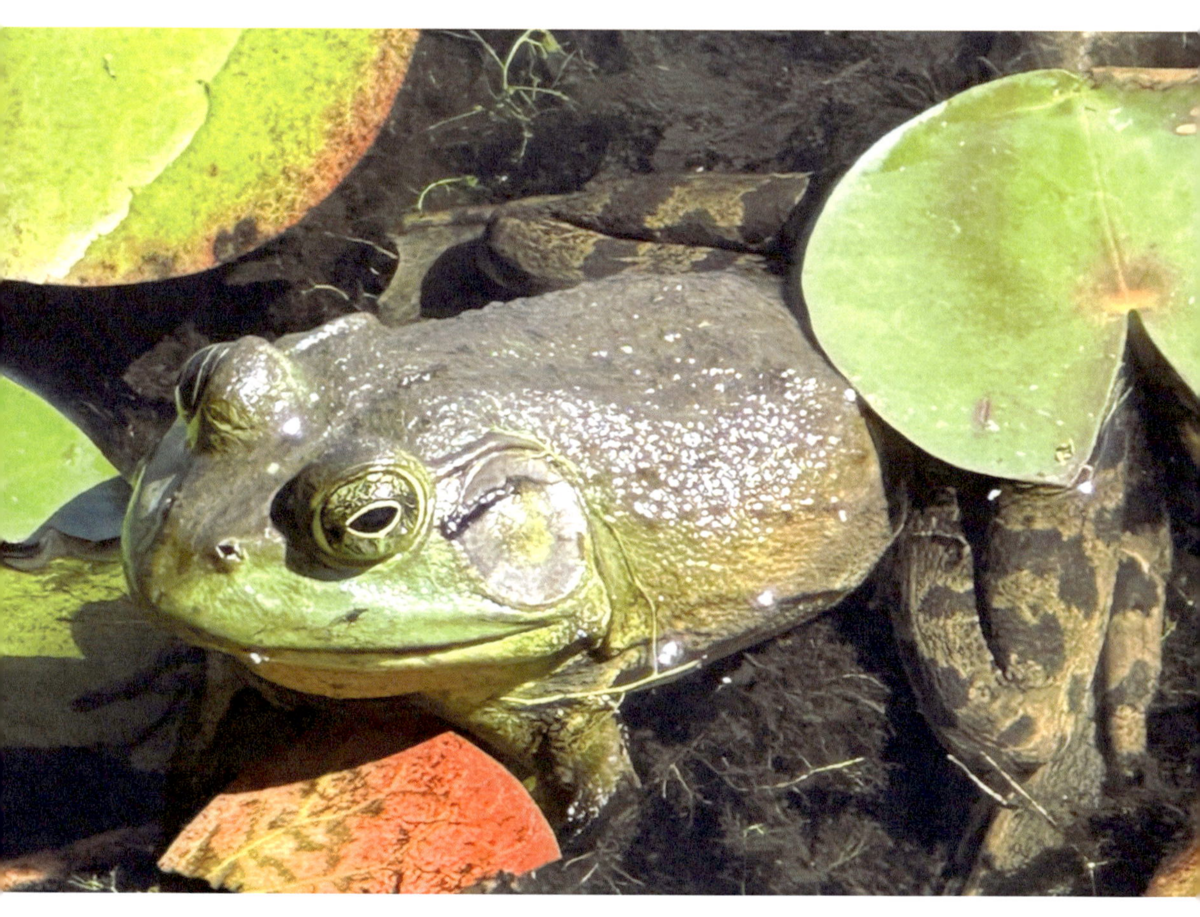

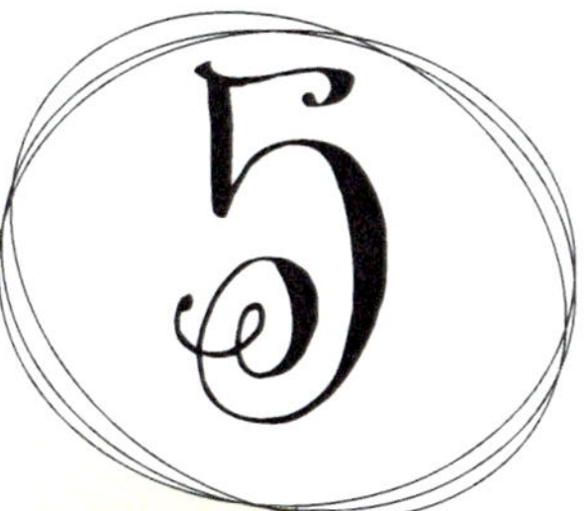

I see beauty in
ordinary things.

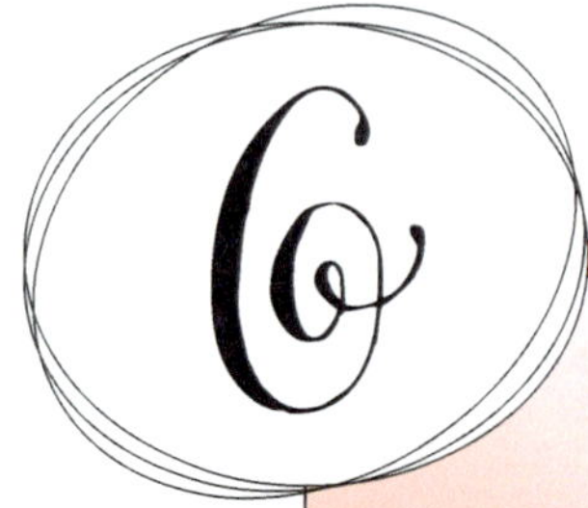

I am kind to strangers.

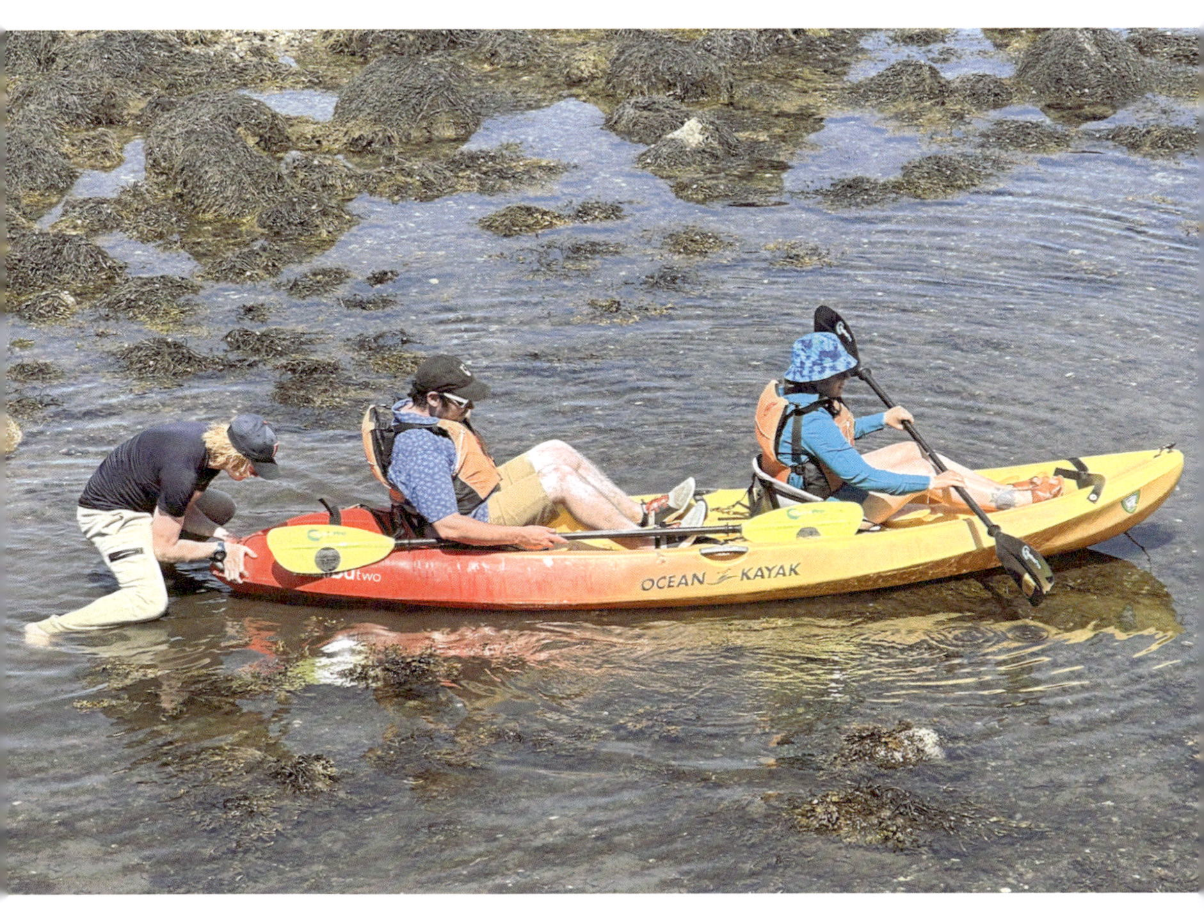

OCEAN KAYAK
two

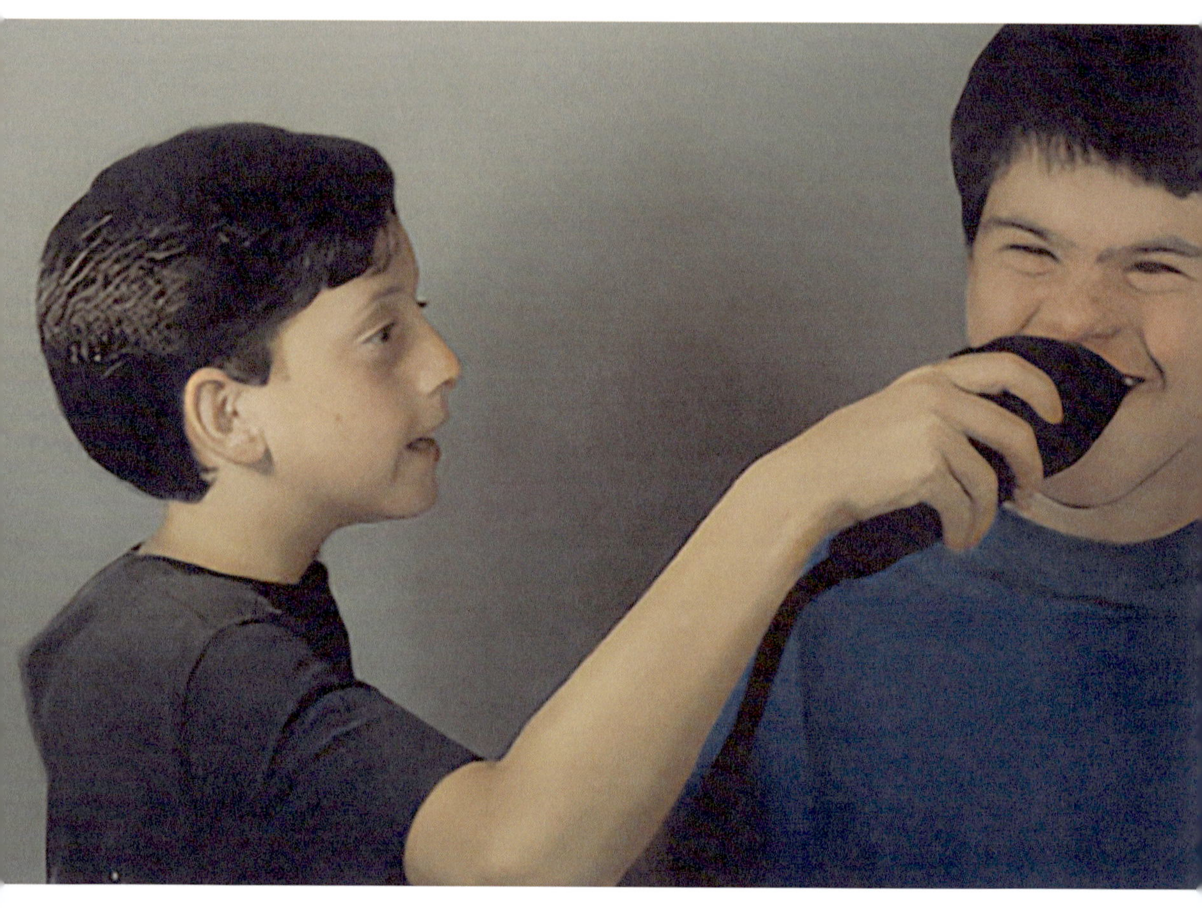

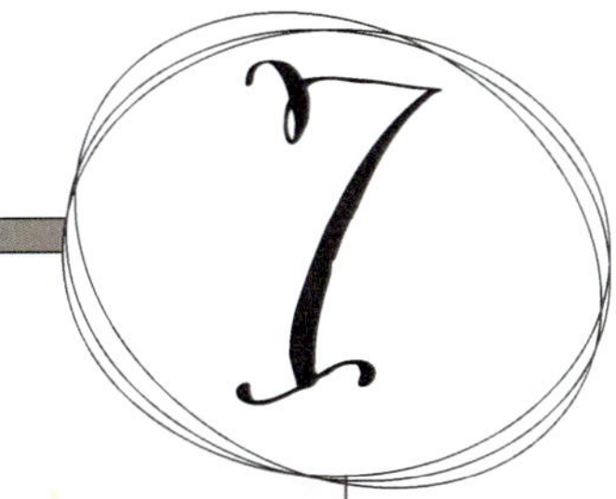

I can laugh at myself.

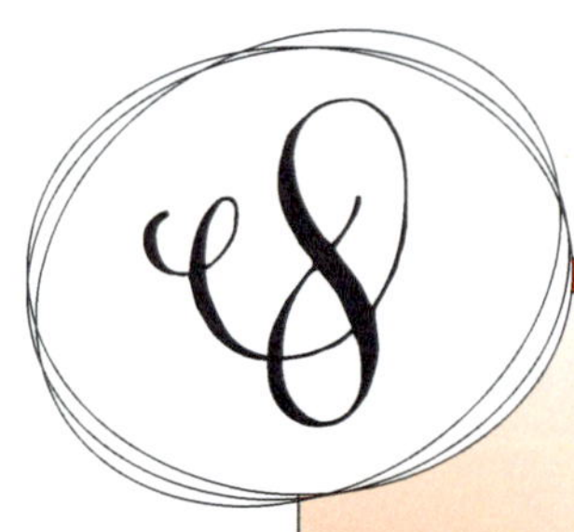

Tomorrow offers infinite possibilities.

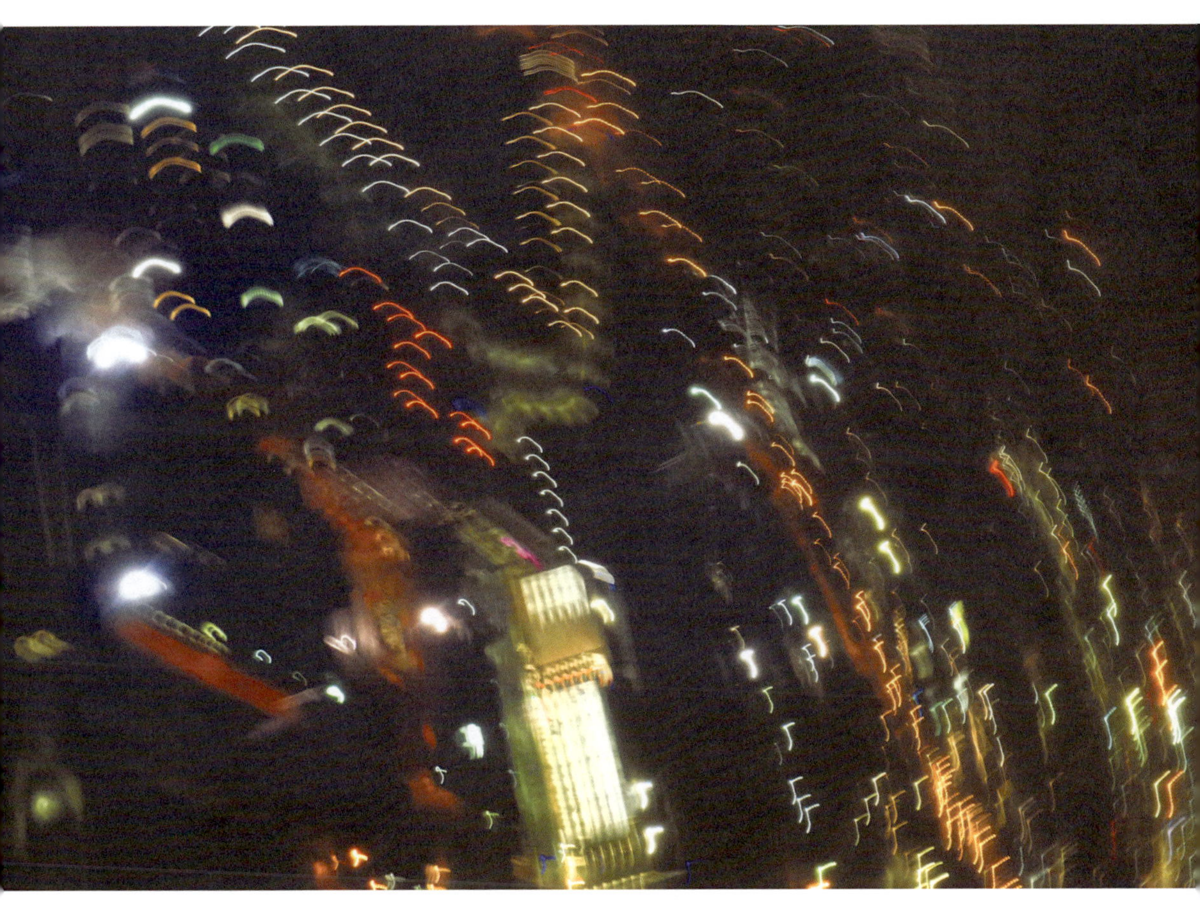

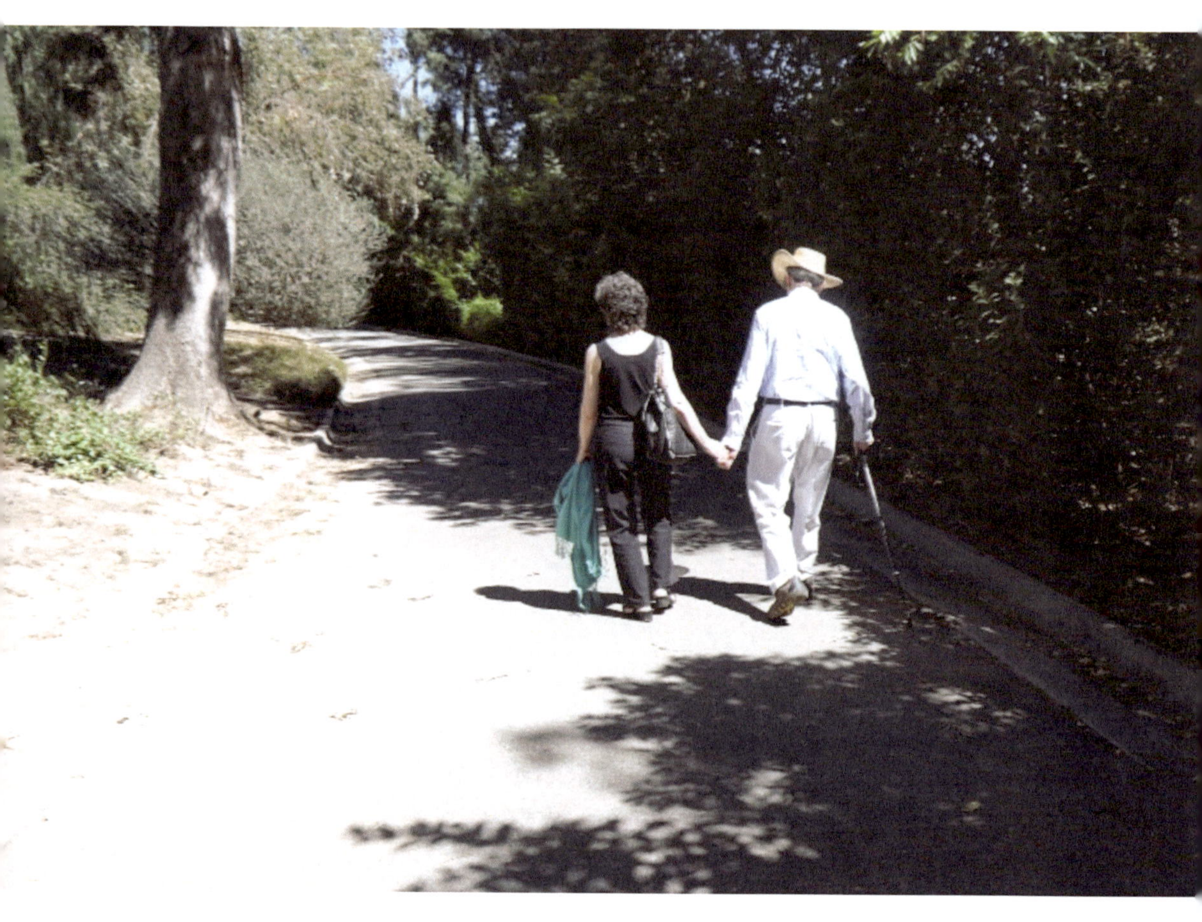

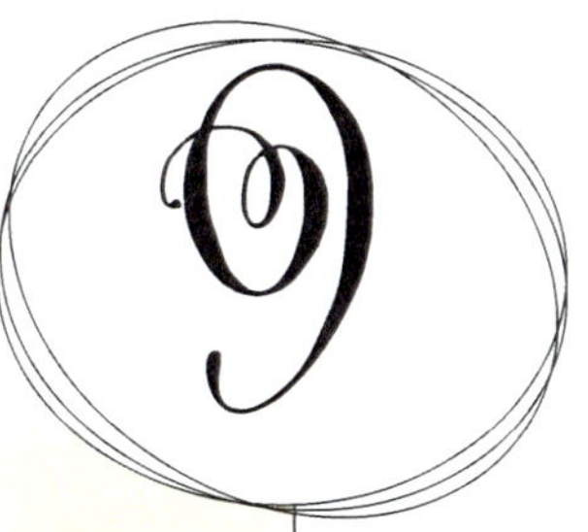

I can call someone I love
to make peace.

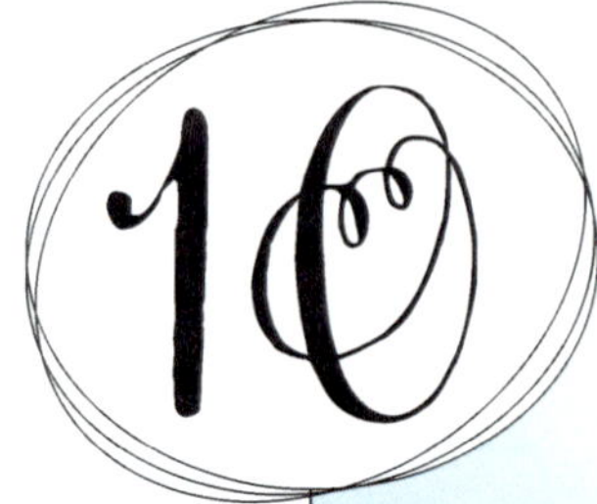

Sleep is a gift.

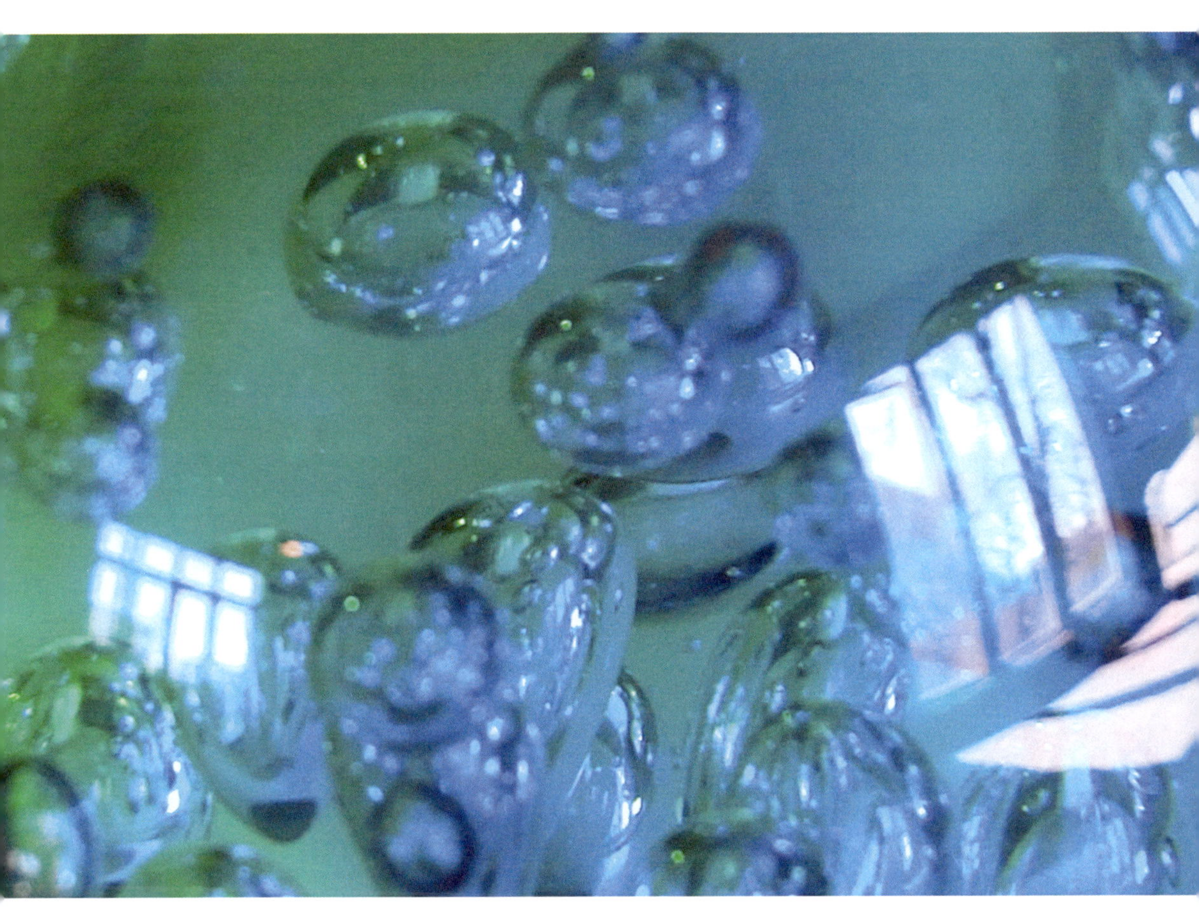

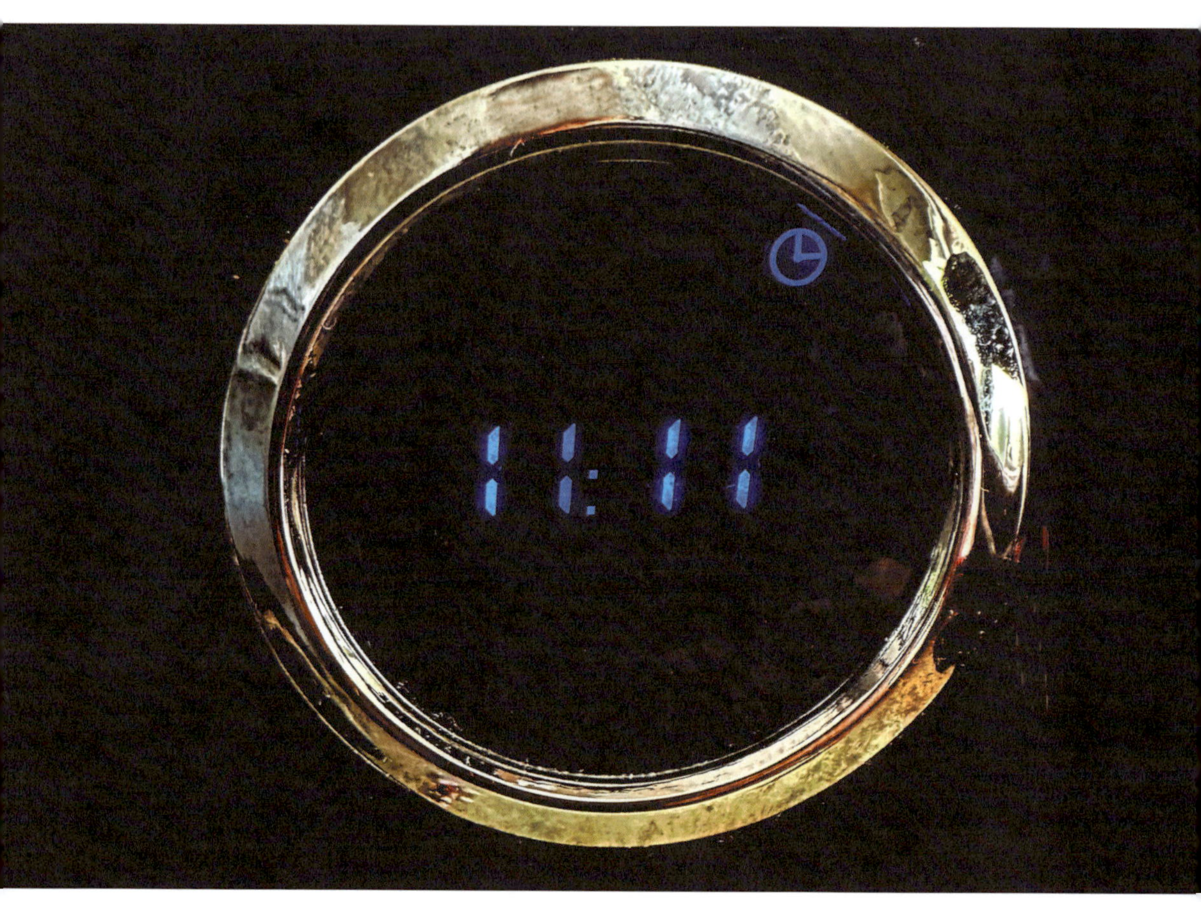

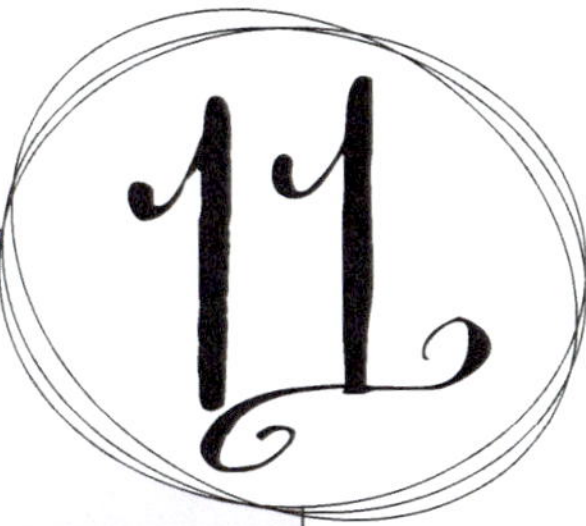

This one is left blank for you to fill in.

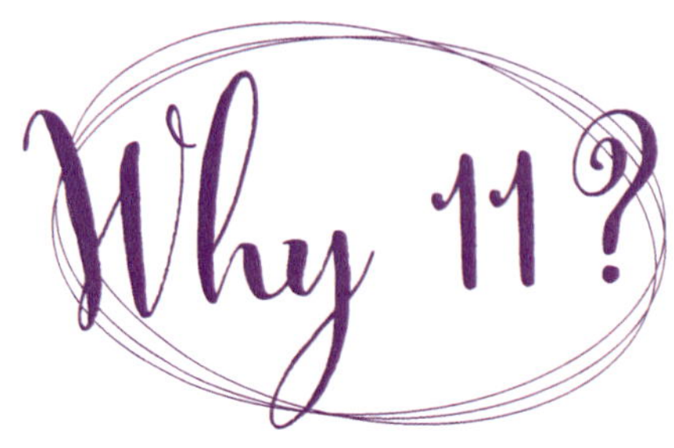

Why 11?

From time immemorial numbers have been crucial to our understanding of the Universe. Aside from their utilitarian value, many individuals believe numbers are equal in importance to words and that, in fact, numbers have a language of their own, complete with syntax and structure, a language that can be mastered and then used as a divining tool. Spiritual teachers from many parts of the world concur that numbers possess mystical qualities that reveal mysteries about our lives and help us to understand our unique place and destiny in the Universe.

There seems to be consensus among spiritual teachers on what the number **11** represents: intuition, knowledge, and enlightenment. In Numerology—the study of the meaning of numbers—one of the ways of determining the unique quality and personality of each person is to add up the numbers of the day, month, and year of their birth. If the final number is **11**, it is believed that people born under this number possess heightened psychic abilities, making them natural healers, teachers, and spiritual channels.

In Astrology, the number **11** is linked to the Zodiac sign of Aquarius, signifying freedom and equality.

The number **11** is a prime number, which means that it can only be divided by itself. In contrast, it reminds us we are not alone and we are not separate. If you look closely, the number **11** actually looks like two people standing next to one another. The number **11** affirms we are all part of the great tapestry of humanity and, when we ignore our instinctive and primordial need for meaningful relationships, we get into trouble as a species.

Here's hoping this book and the **11 Things to Celebrate** series will remind you that we are all partners in this great adventure called Life, and that it is vital to celebrate and express gratitude at all times--but especially when we rise up in the morning and when we lie down at night to sleep…perchance to dream.

About The Author

Ruth Broyde Sharone is a veteran filmmaker, journalist, and author, as well as the creator of the Musical *MEET ME THERE*, —an exuberant celebration of cultural and religious diversity. She wrote, produced, and directed the award-winning documentary *God and Allah Need to Talk*, which has been screened on college campuses across the U.S. and around the world. Her interfaith memoir, *Minefields and Miracles*, received multiple literary awards and more than 30 endorsements from religious leaders, including H.H. the Dalai Lama. Ruth has also contributed over 50 articles to *The Interfaith Observer* and co-authored the 2018 Amazon best-seller, *21st Century Voices: Women Who Influence, Inspire, and Make a Difference.*

InterfaithTheMusical.com

About The Photographer

Leah Broyde Abrahams is a passionate Boston-based visual artist whose work has been juried into numerous exhibitions, including several solo shows. She also served as curator for the videotaped art show *The Telephone Game*, featuring 11 artists from the U.S. and Israel. After a career in program evaluation and research—and leadership in volunteerism in Green Bay, Wisconsin—Leah founded *Mixed Media Memoirs*, a publishing company. She has produced a number of video memoirs and more than 35 books, some of which have won national awards. Today, her primary focus is photography. Her dos-à-dos-bound photobook *Do You See What I See?* was selected for the 2023 National Exhibition of Self-Published Photobooks.

LeahAbrahamsPhotography.com

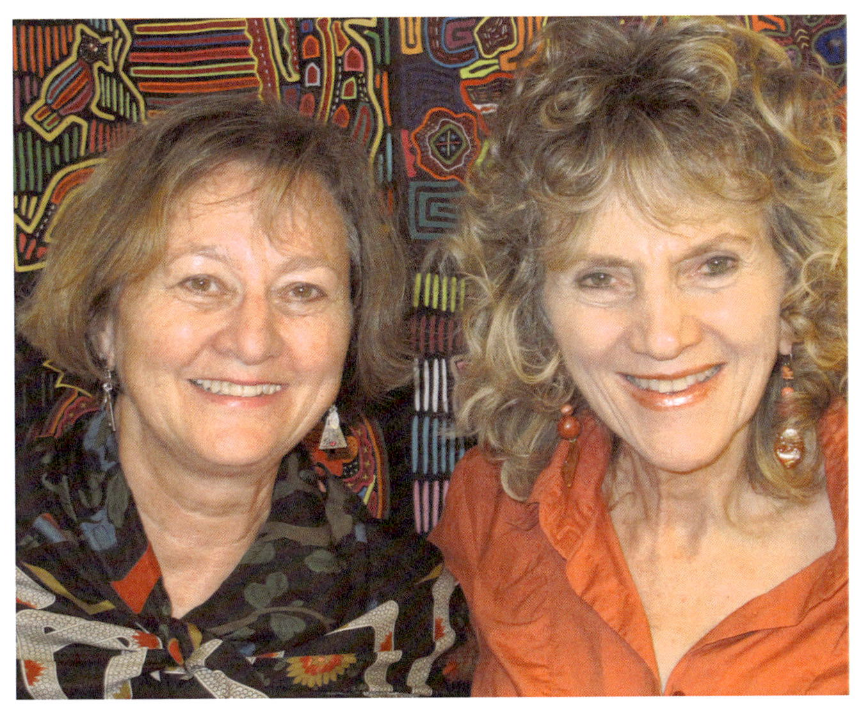

Leah

Ruth

Exciting news!
Our first collaboration in this series, *11 Things to Celebrate Before Breakfast*, was juried into the international 15th Annual Self-Published Photobook Exhibition/2025.

www.ingramcontent.com/pod-product-compliance
Lightning Source LLC
Chambersburg PA
CBRC091244050726
47599CB00009B/984